CREATING FANTASY ART

How To Draw
DARK
FANTASY ART

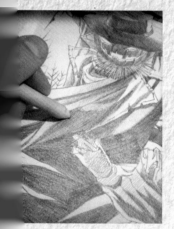

STEVE BEAUMONT

Published in 2018 by
The Rosen Publishing Group, Inc.
29 East 21st Street
New York, NY 10010

Library of Congress Cataloging-in-Publication Data

Names: Beaumont, Steve, author.
Title: How to draw dark fantasy art / Steve Beaumont.
Description: New York : Rosen YA, 2017. | Series: Creating fantasy art | Includes bibliographical references and index.
Identifiers: LCCN 2017003392| ISBN 9781499466690 (library-bound) | ISBN 9781499466720 (pbk.) | ISBN 9781499466676 (6-pack)
Subjects: LCSH: Fantasy in art—Juvenile literature. | Drawing—Technique—Juvenile literature.
Classification: LCC NC825.F25 B415 2017 | DDC 741.2—dc23
LC record available at https://lccn.loc.gov/2017003392

Manufactured in the United States of America

Copyright © 2014 Arcturus Holdings Ltd., 2018

Thanks to the following artists' materials brands that appear in this book: Copic® [Copic is a trademark of Too Corporation in Japan], Derwent, Faber-Castell, Letraset, Staedtler, Winsor & Newton.

All illustrations are original. Credits for additional images: Shutterstock: 19, 20, 28

CONTENTS

GUNSLINGER
Page 14

DARK ANGEL
Page 22

HALLOWEEN
Page 28

INTRODUCTION

What is it about fantasy art that so many find appealing? Is it that it covers so many different genres, from horror and science fiction to swashbuckling, swords and sorcery? Is it that it offers the opportunity to engage with extraordinary characters and creatures in extraordinary worlds? Is it because there are no barriers and that anything is possible? The answer is that it is all of these things, and every individual enjoys different aspects of the genre. In this book we will explore a small collection of some of those characters and the worlds they inhabit and in the process create some exciting fantasy art.

I have had a life-long love affair with comics, books and films dealing with themes of fantasy. As a child, I enjoyed nothing more than reading DC Comics' *Batman* series drawn by Dick Sprang, the first artist to inspire me to produce a piece of fantasy art. Later, motivation was provided by Jack Kirby and Frank Frazetta's art. In my teenage years, Frazetta's work opened up all kinds of possibilities for fantasy drawings, based upon and inspired by my favorite tv shows and films, including *Doctor Who*, *The Outer Limits*, *The Twilight Zone*, *Frankenstein* and *Creature from the Black Lagoon*.

I have been professionally providing illustration, concept art, storyboards and (occasionally) comic-book art for the past 20 years or so. I have had no professional tutoring: everything I have learned has been self-taught, proving that anyone, with practice, can produce fantastic and fantastical art. What I will be passing on to you within the pages of this book are some of the techniques and approaches I have developed, either by accident or by watching other artists at work, over my professional career.

I also teach a "how to draw fantasy art" class and this book incorporates some of the themes and tutorials used there. It is a companion book, if you like. During the years the class has been running, I have successfully enabled a number of students to compile a portfolio of work, which they showed to talent scouts at comic conventions and eventually led to them getting commissions from Marvel Comics. What I will be showing you in the following pages are easy-to-follow steps that will guide you through the process of producing a piece of fantasy art. I have not gone into every minute detail and this is because, as I keep telling my students, I do not want to encourage you to copy my style and exactly how I draw as if it were the only way, as we all have to find our own path forward.

This book is not aimed at the professional or semi-professional artist, it is more for those (the amateur, if you like) who enjoy drawing and are fans of fantasy art and are looking for some tips and ideas that will enable them to take their drawings skills a stage further. I thought it would also be helpful to document any changes I thought of as I went along. Unlike drawings I produce for a client, which are meticulously planned and go through various stages of development, I have approached these artworks as I would any drawing I am producing just for myself – complete with mistakes, experiments and last-minute revisions. I have included these thoughts and alterations in the hope that they will encourage you constantly to seek to improve your work. Remember, it's vital not to worry too much about making mistakes – instead, keep the drawings you are not happy with to remind you what not to do next time.

When I was having fun drawing as a child, I mostly drew from comic books and from what I had seen on tv or at the cinema. Basically, I drew what pleased me and what I was interested in, and this is true of most fantasy artists. For instance, Frank Frazetta is a sports fan and, from what I have read, something of an athlete, and this is evident in his work. Adi Granov has a love of automobiles, aircraft and machinery and these are strong features in his drawings. Claire Wendling clearly has a love, understanding and passion for wildlife and nature. They draw what they are passionate about and this makes them better artists, in my opinion.

Personally, I love horror and sci-fi movies and comics and 70 percent of my daily work is related to these themes. I enjoy working with this subject matter and I hope you find drawing it as fun

and exciting as I do and that it will encourage you to become a better artist.

Have fun!

Steve Beaumont

The prehistoric beast in *Creature from the Black Lagoon*, 1954

Materials

A good artist is able to use their experience and ability to draw something great with even the most basic of tools.

If you ever go to a comic convention and watch artists draw, you will notice that each artist has his or her preferred brand of pen or pencil. I often try out new materials after watching another artist work with a tool that I have not used before.

This section covers some of the tools I have tried and tested and used for the drawings in this book.

PAPER

With so many different surfaces and weights of paper on the market it would be difficult to mention them all here. If I am working in pencil I use a variety of weights and surfaces of cartridge paper, depending on the desired type of pencil line I am trying to achieve.

I can recommend Winsor & Newton cartridge paper. I use 180gsm for general rough sketching and 300gsm for finished artwork. I use a medium rough-surface paper for pencil work that I want to blend, as this gives excellent effects and is also good for dry brushwork when using ink. I use a smooth-surface paper for work requiring a precise, crisp line.

When working with paint, I like to use Langton Prestige Hot Pressed paper 300–400gsm, Saunders Waterford Hot Pressed paper 300–400gsm and Arches Aquarelle Watercolor Paper 300gsm all surfaces. For most brands, the following abbreviations are given: HP = Hot Pressed (smooth finish); NOT/CP = Cold Pressed (slightly textured); Rough Surface = rough.

PENCILS

I depend on a variety of pencils, but the ones I use on a daily basis are the Staedtler Mars Lumograph HB pencil or a Staedtler Noris HB pencil. The Mars Lumograph is a high-quality artist's pencil, while the Noris is more of an office pencil. I also use Faber-Castell Pitt Graphite Pure HB and 6B and Wolff's Carbon pencils, which deliver rich black tones.

Staedtler Mars Lumograph HB pencil (left) and Staedtler Noris HB pencil

BLENDERS AND ERASERS

I sometimes use Derwent paper stumps for blending, but I have also used unbranded and economy blenders to good effect. I use tissue paper wrapped around my finger for some blending situations.

There are many different erasers on the market, but I find Winsor & Newton Kneaded Putty Rubbers and Staedtler plastic erasers to be very reasonable quality.

Staedtler plastic eraser

Winsor & Newton putty rubber

Derwent paper stumps

MARKERS

Marker brands have come and gone in my years as a professional artist. These days I almost exclusively use Copic markers because they offer a flat coverage of ink and a variety of nibs (making them highly versatile); replacement inks and nibs are available. The color range is also impressive. Other brands, such as Prismacolor, also produce high-quality markers, so it is worth exploring and making up your own mind.

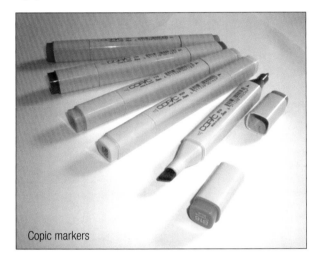

Copic markers

INK PENS

I have been using Faber-Castell Pitt artist pens for a long time now and still like working with them. I also like Copic Multiliners and the Pentel Brush Pen.

Faber-Castell Pitt artist pens

Faber-Castel Pitt artist pens are available in a variety of nib sizes, indicated by the letter or letters on the side of the pen: XS = Extra superfine, S = Superfine, F = Fine, M = Medium and B = Brush.

Copic Multiliner pens are available in a number of nib thicknesses, ranging from 0.03–0.7 to brush. They are refillable and can have their nibs replaced.

Copic Multiliner pens

INK

High-quality India ink is available online and in good craft stores. I work with various brands, including Dr. Ph. Martin's Bombay India Ink, Sennelier Black India Ink (also known as Chinese Ink), Higgins Ink and Stephens Black Drawing Ink.

GOUACHE

When I produce a painted illustration, I normally use gouache as it is a versatile medium and it dries quickly. My preference is Winsor & Newton Designers Gouache, which is very good quality.

BRUSHES

I use Winsor & Newton sable brushes for inking and painting. Sable brushes are expensive, but they last longer than mixed-fiber and nylon brushes, and they also carry more ink and produce a more controllable line.

Winsor & Newton sable brushes

FIGURE DRAWING

Figure drawing can be a huge stumbling block for many beginners and even for some people who have been drawing for a while. When it comes to drawing dragons or other beasts there often appears to be no problem at all, but when a well-balanced figure drawing is required, issues can arise. In the next pages I offer some of the approaches to figure drawing that have helped my students gain more confidence. This section is intended to give a basic overview of the techniques so that they can be applied assuredly to imaginative drawings.

BASIC ANATOMY

Humans come in all shapes and sizes and with all kinds of variations that make each one unique, but for the purpose of getting started on producing a balanced and well-proportioned figure, let's look at the basic, muscular, human form. As a rough guide, the adult human form is about seven-and-a-half heads tall. However, it is common practice to exaggerate the proportions of fantasy characters, and the imagined figure is more usually eight-and-three-quarters heads tall, whether it is male or female (Figure 1). I, as well as my students, have found it helpful to have a rough knowledge of the skeletal structure of our bodies. I can draw a figure better if I understand how it should look and how it works, otherwise I am merely guessing and filling in the vague areas using incomplete information, which will be evident in the end result. The human skeleton comprises about 206 bones, some of which are labelled in Figure 2.

Memorizing the names for each and every bone is not essential for successful figure drawing, but it is helpful to be familiar with the names, proportions and joint structures of ones that are most important for drawing the human form. It would take far too long to draw a complete skeleton every time you wanted to draw a figure and, moreover, it is not necessary. Instead, you can simply break down the skeleton into some basic, manageable shapes or lines and this should enable you to achieve some pleasing results.

Figure 1

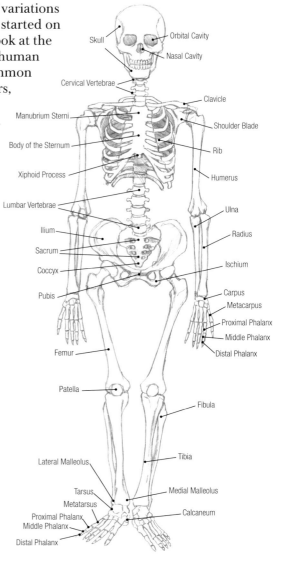

Figure 2

Skull · Orbital Cavity · Nasal Cavity · Cervical Vertebrae · Manubrium Sterni · Body of the Sternum · Xiphoid Process · Lumbar Vertebrae · Ilium · Sacrum · Coccyx · Pubis · Femur · Patella · Lateral Malleolus · Tarsus · Metatarsus · Proximal Phalanx · Middle Phalanx · Distal Phalanx · Clavicle · Shoulder Blade · Rib · Humerus · Ulna · Radius · Ischium · Carpus · Metacarpus · Proximal Phalanx · Middle Phalanx · Distal Phalanx · Fibula · Tibia · Medial Malleolus · Calcaneum

BREAKING DOWN THE FIGURE

My students have achieved good results with three approaches to figure drawing. Some students responded well to stripping down the skeleton to a simplified stick form as shown in Figure 3, while others had more success using construction shapes – an assortment of ovals, cylinders and spheres – to construct a figure, as shown in Figure 4. I personally go about figure drawing by loosely sketching the form and feeling my way around the shape as I go along, as shown in Figure 5, and some students have also found using this approach useful. With all these methods, the main points to keep in mind are the size of the head in relation to the body and the length and position of the arms and legs. The arms can be divided into two roughly equal lengths. The torso can be put together using an oval (I sometimes draw a shape that resembles a rib cage, as in Figure 5) for the rib cage and a shape resembling a pair of briefs for the pelvis.

Figure 3   **Figure 4**

It is good practice to study yourself in the mirror – preferably a full-length one – to become aware of how certain poses affect parts of the body. For example, try standing with both legs straight with your bodyweight centered over them, then transfer your bodyweight to just one leg. Notice the effect this movement has on the other leg. What has happened to the stance? What differences do you notice? Has the shift of weight affected other parts of the body, such as the pelvis, your shoulders or the curve of your back and spine? What about the angle of your head? Recreating what you see in the mirror in your figure drawing will make the artwork that much more convincing. (You could take a photo of your reflection in a certain stance to refer to while you are drawing.)

Figures 3-6 are examples of how the different methods can be used to create a dynamic pose. Sometimes it helps to think about the direction of the twists and turns within a pose to help capture the movement, and these forces can be indicated by arrows, as in Figure 3.

Figure 5   **Figure 6**

DRAWING THE HEAD

Drawing the head need not be a difficult task. If you think of the skull as a sphere with sections removed from either side (Figure 1) and a roughly cubed shape attached to one of the bottom quarters then you will be able to create the basic shape (Figure 2). If you look at the sphere from the side and divide it into quarters, the center line is roughly where the eyes sit. If you continue a line from the bottom of the sphere, it will mark the position of the bottom of the nose. The jaw line runs at an angle away from the bottom of the sphere. If you mark a line between the nose and the bottom of the jaw, you will have the position of the mouth (Figure 3).

This technique gives you the guidelines for positioning simple features in the correct place (Figure 4). You now need to practice drawing the features themselves, whether by looking in a mirror or by doing the exercises in this book. With patience and practice, you will perfect your technique and the curves and shapes of features such as the eyes, nose and mouth will come naturally.

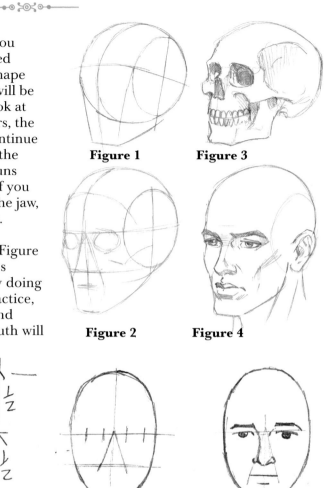

Figure 1   **Figure 3**

Figure 2   **Figure 4**

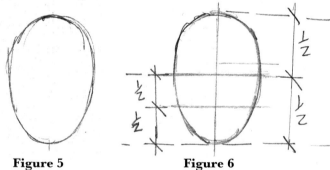

Figure 5   **Figure 6**

Figure 7   **Figure 8**

If, however, you are struggling to use the ball and cube technique, there is an alternative, simpler approach you could try. Draw an oval (Figure 5). Remember what I said earlier about being too technical about initial shapes – just sketch some ovals and divide them into quarters (Figure 6). The central horizontal line is where the eyes should sit. Now draw a line between the center line and the bottom of the oval. This is where the bottom of the nose will come to. Draw a line between the nose and the bottom of the oval. This is where the mouth will sit.

As a rough guide for positioning the eyes, divide the face widthways into five equal parts; the second and fourth space will give you the position of each eye (Figure 7). To work out the width of the nose and mouth, draw two diagonal lines from the bridge of the nose, between the eyes, down towards the bottom of the oval. The points where the diagonal lines cross the line for the mouth denote the outer edges of mouth (Figure 8). Of course, these are just rough guidelines for you to follow. Once you feel more confident about drawing the face, you will be able to create many different shapes and sizes of faces.

Figure 9 shows how just a few simple lines can be used to convey different expressions.

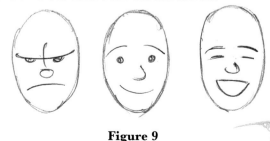

Figure 9

Figures 10–15 show a more detailed breakdown of how to draw the head and face. More often than not I use an oval (Figure 13) for the head. If I am drawing a three-quarters view I may use the structure shown in Figure 1.

As usual, I have divided the width of the face into five equal parts (Figure 11) to give me the position for the eyes, so that they are not too far apart or too close together. To gauge the width of the nose and mouth I draw a triangular shape from the bridge of the nose (Figure 12). This should not be too precise or rigid – some of the things that make a face interesting are the features which do not adhere to the generic grid. Once you become more skilled at drawing faces, you will naturally begin to have fun slightly distorting the proportions.

When drawing hair, I go for uncomplicated shapes that complement the face and look natural (Figure 13), as I find this gives the best result. I am influenced by the way Disney artists draw hair in animated feature films, such as the 1995 film *Pocahontas* which has some lovely stylized flowing hair that I often incorporate into my drawing.

With all the workings-out still prominent, the face is not looking especially attractive. Remove the guidelines and begin to soften the features, making the eyes, nose and mouth prominent (Figure 14). Notice that I have reduced the amount of lines for the nose. It is best to keep line work on faces simple – heavy work around the nose can age the character. Sometimes defining the nose by drawing a simple line, as if the face is being lit from one side, is all that is required. When drawing the female face, use soft curves for the eyelids, lashes and mouth.

You can now shade in the hair (Figure 15), keeping the line work simple and leaving white highlights to give the impression that the hair is glossy. Once you are happy with the drawing, carefully erase all the guidelines and add any final touches to the shading.

Figure 10

Figure 11

Figure 12

Figure 13

Figure 14

Figure 15

PERSPECTIVE

There are so many subtleties when it comes to drawing perspective that it is impossible to cover everything here, but there are some basics you will need in order to follow the exercises in this book. If you want to develop the use of perspective in your drawings then I recommend you purchase a book that focuses purely on it. There are plenty of good ones out there.

The most common example of perspective is single or one-point perspective (Figure 1), which gives an impression of depth. Looking at the cube straight on you can see that the sides on the top seem to draw closer together the further back they go. If these converging lines are extended beyond the back edge of the cube they will eventually meet at what is called the vanishing point. The level at which they meet is the horizon or "eye line." This single-point perspective can also be seen in Figure 2. Notice how the road narrows in the distance towards the horizon. The same would occur in a picture of a railway track or canal.

While single-point perspective deals with the foreshortening of one dimension of an object, two-point perspective deals with the foreshortening of two dimensions and gives an indication of the width of the object along both visible sides. This occurs when a corner point faces the front (Figure 3). If the perspective lines are extended, they eventually meet at two vanishing points on the horizon.

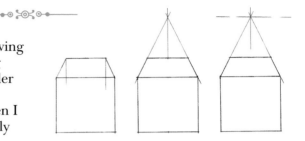

Figure 1

Figure 2

Figure 4

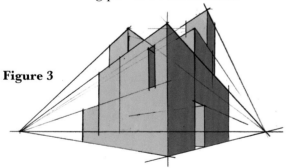

Figure 3

Three-point perspective deals with the foreshortening of three dimensions of an object and occurs when the viewpoint is close to the object, looking up. The third perspective point is a vertical one and it gives the impression of height. Using three-point perspective will enable you to draw dramatic structures, such as the one in Figure 4.

LÍGHTÍNG

Understanding light and shade and where to place highlights and darkened areas can make or break a good piece of illustration. Figure 1 shows how the position of an object in relation to a light source affects the shadow cast by the object. I learned about shading in relation to light by drawing an object lit by a single light source, the position of which changed in each sketch (Figure 2). This simple technique helped me develop an understanding of how light affects a picture. Face A is lit by a soft front-on light source. Face B is lit by a light source to the side of the head, face C is lit by a low light and face D is lit from above.

Of course, lighting is a lot more complex than it appears in these examples and there is often more than one source. In addition, in a confined space a single light source can bounce off the surrounding walls to create additional light sources.

Figure 1

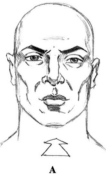

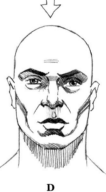

A   B   C   D

Gunslinger

I'm a big fan of both western and horror films. Here I want to look at mixing the two genres. I thought it would be interesting to combine the undead and gunslinger themes and create a zombie cowboy, back from the grave to seek vengeance.

Figure 1

Figure 2

Figure 3

While producing the thumbnails for this picture, I considered a few wide shots showing a full pose (Figure 1, Figure 2 and Figure 3), and I thought about whether to color it or not. In the end I decided to go for a close-up black and white image (Figure 4) as I thought it would be more fun developing the face than drawing a distant, less detailed view.

Figure 4

STEP 1

Map out the figure in rough. You may not need to start with a skeletal figure for this exercise – just gauge the proportions of the arms in relation to the torso. Mark out the dividing lines for the face, which will help you place the eyes, nose and mouth correctly.

STEP 2

Map out the clothing and the skull. When drawing the skull, refer back to page 10 or use the photo reference below (Figure 5), although in the drawing the skull will have withered skin stretched over it. The clothing is based on the long coats worn in Western movies (Figure 6).

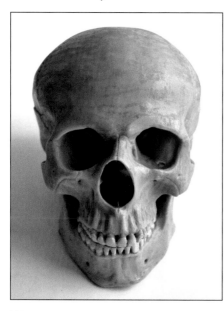

Figure 5

Figure 6

DRAWING THE GUN: PRACTICE

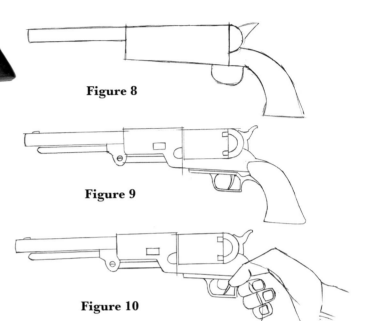

Figure 7

To draw guns successfully it is best to do some research first. Handguns come in all shapes and sizes, from revolvers to automatics, and each has its own characteristics. The gun in this drawing is a Colt Model 1848 Percussion Revolver (Figure 7). As with drawing anything for the first time, I recommend breaking the object down into manageable shapes. This helps you become familiar with the item, making it easier to draw it well.

First establish the basic shape (Figure 8), then add a little more detail to the gun (Figure 9).

Once you are happy with the gun, work out how the hand fits around the handle and trigger (Figure 10).

Figure 8

Figure 9

Figure 10

STEP 3

Once you are familiar with the shape of the gun, go through the stages again with the gun shown in the correct position for the final drawing. Start with the basic shape, then add the leading lever and cylinder pin. Draw in the shape of the hand as it holds the gun, then refine and develop it and add the nails.

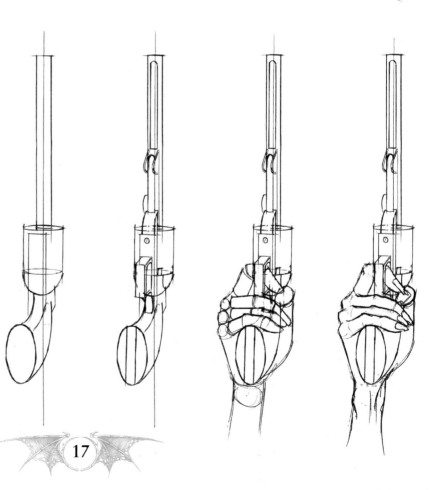

STEP 4

Sketch out the position of the hat, using reference material for a guide to its look (Figure 11), and work out how it sits on the head. Incorrect positioning can look awkward and lopsided, so it is good practice to draw the head and hat as transparent shapes, which can easily be deleted, to get the correct fit. The clothes can also now be developed further.

Figure 11

STEP 5

Remove any development sketch lines with an eraser. Do not worry about making the drawing too clean, as most of the line work will be covered by the shading. Define the features with clean line work, making sure all the details are present for the face, clothing and guns before you commence on the shading.

STEP 6

The first stage of shading is to identify the main solid areas of shadow created by the light source, which in this instance comes from an area to the figure's right as we are looking at him. Block these in using an HB pencil.

STEP 7

Add the mid-range tones with an HB pencil, then softly blend between the dark and mid-range tones with tissue paper (Figure 12). I also used a blending stump around the face. The bullet holes can be strengthened with darker shading.

Figure 12

STEP 8

Bloodstains can be created around the bullet holes by adding a heavy tone with a B pencil, then blending with a blending stump.

STEP 9

The withered skin can now be applied to the skull. It needs to look dried, stretched and drained of all fluids. Wrinkles should be added using the fine point of an HB pencil, which can then be blended with a stump before a further layer of fine detail is applied over the top.

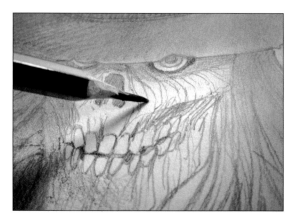

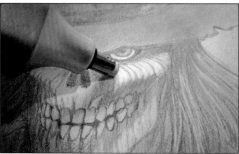

Figure 13

STEP 10

The same process is used for the hands and hair. Using an eraser, create highlights on the hair, face (Figure 13) and hand (Figure 14). Carefully apply a few sparing highlights to the rim of the hat, and to the left edges of the gun barrel, cylinder and trigger guard. Finally, apply a crisp, thin, hard line with a sharp HB pencil to add definition. The completed Gunslinger is on the opposite page.

Figure 14

DARK ANGEL

For this drawing, I drew inspiration from a couple of movies I like that look at themes of urban crime. I liked the idea of creating a drawing that was the polar opposite of conventional angelic imagery, replacing white dove-like wings with huge black crow-like wings, and a black leather/PVC look as opposed to a flowing white gown. The tutu suggests she is some kind of grungy gothic version of the black swan from the ballet *Swan Lake*, with chunky boots instead of ballet shoes.

Figure 1

Figure 2

Start by collating some photo reference material (Figures 1 to 4) to provide inspiration and enable you to draw features such as wings and PVC clothing correctly.

Figure 3

STEP 1

Having developed your skills with the beginner's exercises you may be able to skip the stage when you draw a skeletal frame, jumping instead straight to fleshing out the basic shape, as I have done. Once you are happy that the pose and proportions are correct, roughly sketch out the shape of the wings; there is a diagram of a bird's wing on page 24.

Figure 4

STEP 2

Start to develop the face and
define the body shape. Roughly
sketch the shape of the tutu.
At this stage the hair has been
kept to a simple shape that will be
developed later.

STEP 3

To make the appearance of the wings more realistic
it is a good idea to look closely at various types of
bird's wings. Figure 6 is a diagram of the basic layout
of feathers. It is not essential for you to be familiar
with bird anatomy or to be an expert on wings, but a
general understanding of their construction will help
you to achieve a sense of realism. I have based the
wings loosely on those of a crow or raven, taking the
basic construction and applying some artistic licence
to create a more symmetrical shape. The wings now
appear to be a hybrid of angel's and crow's wings.

Underside of wing

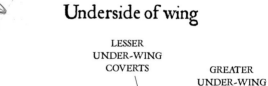

LESSER
UNDER-WING
COVERTS

GREATER
UNDER-WING
COVERTS

Figure 6

PRIMARIES

SECONDARIES

STEP 4

It is now time to add the base tone to the body. The appearance of this figure will be mostly dark tones, so I applied an overall dark base tone with an HB pencil, leaving areas on the upper body and upper legs untouched, as these will have a very light tone applied once the blending has been done.

ADDING DETAIL TO THE FACE, EYES AND HAIR

When constructing a young adult female's face it is important to keep the line work simple. To create an eerie, supernatural effect I left the eyes white, with no pupils or irises, and to make them stand out more I added heavy shading around the eye region (Figure 7).

To create the hair, work from the crown of the head outwards and downwards to form a simple outline (Figure 8). Block in shading, leaving white areas where the highlights are going to be (Figure 9), then blend the pencil work and reinstate highlights as necessary with an eraser (Figure 10).

Figure 7

Figure 8

Figure 9

Figure 10

STEP 5

The pencil work needs to be blended. I wanted a softer effect than I could achieve with a blending stump so I used some tissue paper (Figure 11).

Figure 11

STEP 6

As this is a dark character, I felt that it would be appropriate to frame her against a background of dark clouds. To create the clouds, draw a very light outline of their position, leaving a white area behind the figure so that she stands out, then add a dark base tone to the clouds. This should then be blended and the edges of the clouds softened and shaped with an eraser.

Other finishing touches can now be made. I used the fine edge of an eraser to highlight the feathers, and added highlights to the barbed wire and smaller folds in the material with a fine brush and some permanent white gouache. When creating highlights for a highly reflective surface such as PVC or patent leather, you will need to aim for really dark tones, or even solid black and harsh white highlights, as shown in Figure 5.

STEP 7

To finish the tutu, draw pencil lines from the hip area outwards towards the edge of the paper. The pencil work can then be blended together and some further darker pencil work laid over the top to create a ruffled effect. Use an eraser to create ragged outer edges, cutting back into the tutu in an uneven manner.

The pencil work for the wings should be gently blended together before the highlights are added. The feathers and other detailed areas such as the barbed wire can then be clearly defined with a sharp pencil to create a crisp line.

After completing the drawing I scanned it and then
imported it into Photoshop, where I adjusted the hue
to give it a bluish tone. This gives the final image a
moody atmosphere and adds impact.

HALLOWEEN

As a child, I was taken to see Walt Disney's animated feature film, *The Adventures of Ichabod and Mr Toad* (1949), which contains the tale of *The Legend of Sleepy Hollow*. I loved the story and imagery of Ichabod Crane and the headless horseman. Imagery from the film informs this drawing, as well as references from other sources and, of course, my imagination.

Initially, this character was going to be a creepy looking scarecrow that had been brought to life to terrorize a remote run-down farm with a rusty but lethal sickle. I sketched a few ideas of a sack-headed scarecrow (Figure 1), which I thought had some merit, but I decided they looked too much like the DC Comics character The Scarecrow, one of Batman's well-known adversaries. So I changed tack and developed a series of thumbnail sketches of a pumpkin-headed scarecrow in order to find the right content and layout.

Figure 1

The first ideas I developed depicted a scarecrow terrorizing a young farm boy (Figure 2). Although I liked these, I was not completely satisfied with the tone and atmosphere. Then I remembered a famous film poster that shows a simple yet striking image of the central character, wielding a weapon above his head in a field of crops. Nothing else – no other people in the shot. I realized that the power of the image was derived from the uninterrupted connection between the character and the viewer, and that by removing the figure in the foreground of my drawing I would be able to create a similarly strong link.

Figure 2

Figure 3

Figure 4

With this in mind, I developed two more thumbnail sketches (Figures 3 and 4), which I felt worked much better. I really liked the wide shot (Figure 3), which allowed me to introduce background details such as the barn and to recreate the atmosphere of the poster. However, I eventually decided on the tighter shot (Figure 4), as it draws the viewer closer to the menacing scarecrow.

Before developing the final drawing I explored a few styles of pumpkin head to see which had the right creepy vibe (Figure 5). I thought jagged teeth would look scary, but once I had drawn them I felt they looked a bit clichéd. I decided in the end to go for a classic Halloween pumpkin, which was more understated but created the visual I was looking for. You may want to give your pumpkin jagged teeth – as with most details when drawing, there is no such thing as right or wrong and it all comes down to personal preference.

Figure 5

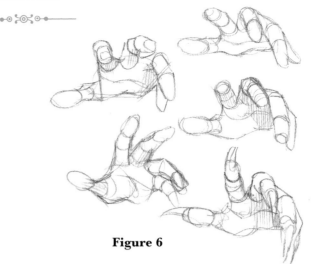

Figure 6

STEP 1

As the artwork has a central composition, it makes sense to plot the drawing around a center line. I roughly marked out the shape the crops would make (Step 1). You will notice that this echoes the shape of the sun.

I wasn't completely satisfied with the hand reaching out that I had drawn in the original thumbnail sketch. I therefore held my hand in various positions and used a mirror to see how it looked, then drew a series of sketches (Figure 6) so that I could assess which pose would work best.

STEP 2

Start filling in the details, sketching the crops before you begin work on the figure. I drew the stalks coming into the frame from the outer edges of the paper, growing less dense as they reach the center. It may look as though I have drawn a lot of randomly placed leaves, but when you shade in the picture you will notice that their arrangement creates a dark, shadowy space in the middle that draws your eye to the scarecrow.

For the clothing, I chose to draw a tatty overcoat, scarf and hat, the style and details of which are obscured by the rips, tears and general dirtiness of the garments. The gloves are workman's gloves – the type a farmer or construction worker might wear.

The clothing is baggy and the skeletal structure of the scarecrow is based on a wooden cross-shaped frame rather than a human body. I wanted the arms to be long and thin, this creates a creepy, skeleton impression.

STEP 3

Having plotted the drawing, take a step back and assess it. When I studied my drawing, the raised arm holding the sickle caught my eye straight away; everything about it just looked wrong. I went and replicated the pose in a mirror and found that the position of the arm was not correct. After studying the pose carefully, I returned to my desk and practiced redrawing the arm on scrap paper before amending my drawing (Figure 7).

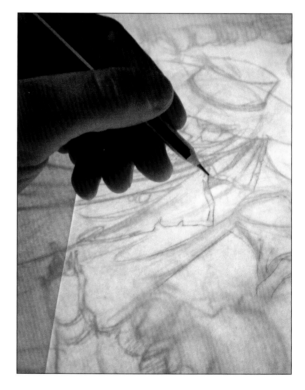

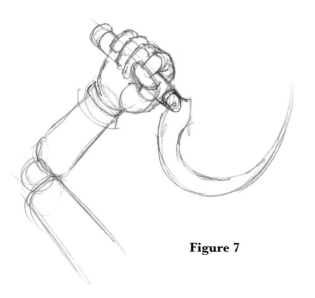

Figure 7

STEP 4

Check the drawing one more time, then trace the image on to a sheet of cartridge paper using a pencil and a lightbox, if you have one. You should now have a clean, accurate outline to work to (Figure 8, opposite).

Figure 8

STEP 5

Using a Palomino Blackwing 602, darken the areas that will give the image its strength and weight. You may notice in my drawing that the darkened areas run up the center of the page, creating a linear design. This is a deliberate device to make sure the viewer's eye does not wander away from the main point of interest.

STEP 6

Use a blending stump to achieve a smoother, more opaque finish on the darker areas of shading. Figure 9 on the facing page shows the finished result. As a pencil drawing, this artwork is now complete. However, you can take it a stage further and add color, as I have done, if you like.

Figure 9

STEP 7

Scan the drawing and import it into Photoshop. Apply a first layer of base color using the Fill option, set to Multiply. Here, I used a very pale warm yellow as a foundation for the warm tones.

I added color to the sky in three layers. The first of these was a deep orange, over which I placed another layer of deep red, followed by a layer of dull red with a percentage of black in it to create the darker tones at the top. All the layers were set to Multiply. I mainly used just one brush to apply the coloring. This is a customized brush I created from a pencil rubbing (Figure 10), but it is likely that there are similar brushes available on the Internet that you can download for free.

Figure 10

STEP 8

On another layer, apply a rich deep orange for the sun. Use the same orange for the rest of the image, but put it on a separate layer in case you need to adjust the opacity to blend with the olive tones that are going to be added. Both layers should be set to Multiply.

Figure 11

STEP 9

Begin to build up the colors for the crops using layers of olive green. In this step picture I have deselected the orange layer, shown in Step 8, so you can get an idea of the tone of the green, but you don't need to do this. I have merged the green with the outline of the scarecrow in order to create a subtle tonal blend as I apply other colors. All layers are set to Multiply.

I have returned the orange layer in Figure 11 to show how the color blends with the olive greens, creating rustic and darker tones.

STEP 10

Enlarge the diameter of the brush tool, zoom in and dab the olive green over details such as the leaves to create textural detail and interest.

STEP 11

On another layer, using the same brush and a dark warm grey, apply texture to the scarecrow's clothing. With the layer set to Multiply, create a denser grouping of strokes to create darker tones.

STEP 12

Create the darkest tones using a dark warm grey that is about 25 percent lighter than a solid black. I applied this to the scarecrow, the really dark areas of the crops at the bottom of the picture and to the silhouetted crops in the background.

STEP 13

On the top layer, apply yellow and light orange highlights to the scarecrow to make him stand out even more from the darkened background. The highlights should be set to Normal rather than Multiply (meaning they are opaque rather than transparent). Use highlights to pick out the gloved hand reaching towards the viewer and on the clothing and straw hat, both of which have light cast on them from the glowing pumpkin head.

SKETCHBOOK

I often stress the importance of keeping sketchbooks to my students. They can be used for any kind of drawing – from observational sketches or the exploration of ideas to testing out new materials (pens, pencils, paints, etc.) or just doodling for the fun of it. All these activities help to develop drawing skills and, as with most things, the more you practice, the better you become.

   Professional artists fill dozens of sketchbooks. The rough workings of some, including Frank Frazetta, Jeffrey Jones and Claire Wendling, have been turned into high-end art books that showcase their creative processes. The seeds of some of your best ideas may be doodled in a sketchbook. Ideas flow uninhibited when you are not feeling too precious about your drawing and you may often experience a breakthrough in this way.

When I recently undertook a project for drawing a dragon I had so many ideas fighting to get out that I had to spend a bit of time rough-sketching all kinds of dragons and layouts in order to unclutter my head. It was also fun just to play around with shapes and capture movement, and it reminded me how enjoyable sketching can be. When I came to break down the composition, however, I realized that such a detailed design would require too much space, so I opted for a simpler, more conventional design.

GLOSSARY

anatomy The body structure of humans and animals.

composition The way that different elements are set together to create an overall effect.

distorted Pulled and twisted out of shape.

genre A style of film, art, music or literature.

gouache Paint with a glue-like texture.

hybrid Something made by combining two separate elements.

lightbox A flat box with a translucent top and light inside, used by artists to help when tracing pictures.

pose The way that a person stands.

realism A way of representing something in art so that it looks real.

symmetrical The same on both sides of a central line.

FURTHER INFORMATION

Chris Riddell's Doodle-a-Day by Chris Riddell (Macmillan Children's Books, 2015)

Draw and Write Your Own Comics by Louie Stowell (Usborne Publishing, 2014)

Drawing Fantasy Creatures by Aaron Sautter (Capstone Press, 2016)

Drawing Manga: Step-by-Step by Ben Krefta (Arcturus Publishing, 2013)

Drawing Wizards, Witches and Warlocks by Christ Hart (Sixth and Spring Books, 2009)

How to Draw Fantasy Art by Mark Bergin (PowerKids Press, 2011)

Terry Pratchett's Discworld Colouring Book by Paul Kidby (Gollancz, 2016)

INDEX